# 555 Powerful Leadership Coaching Questions

## Mastering Leadership and Coaching with Powerful Questions to Inspire Growth and Drive Performance

Be.Bull Publishing Group
Mauricio Vasquez

Toronto, Canada

Authors:

Mauricio Vasquez
Be.Bull Publishing Group

First Printing: June 2024

ISBN 978-1-998402-53-3 (Paperback)
ISBN 978-1-998402-54-0 (Hardcover)
ISBN 978-1-998402-55-7 (Ebook)

**Dear Valued Reader,**

We kindly ask for your support in leaving a review for our book. Unlike large publishing companies, we rely heavily on the feedback of readers like you.

Your review will not only help us improve and reach more readers, but it will also allow you to share your insights and experiences, contributing to a community of like-minded individuals who are passionate about leadership and personal growth.

To leave your review, please scan the QR code provided.

Your input is invaluable to us, and we thank you in advance for your support!

Warm regards,

Mauricio Vasquez
Be.Bull Publishing

# INTRODUCTION

Asking questions is, has been, and always will be part of our nature. Questions allow us to gather information, learn new things, and strengthen our relationships with others in unique ways.

Why is asking powerful and insightful questions important for your work and life?

Foremost, asking questions and really listening to others shows that you truly care. When you are at work, and you ask powerful questions to your colleagues, they will then know that you value them and care about their needs and opinions. Your interactions with them will always be more successful and gratifying when you are honest and intentional in acknowledging their actual needs, knowledge, and opinions.

Asking questions will allow you to align your or your organization's goals and strategies with your colleagues' objectives, priorities, and needs, and vice versa. This needs to be done with understanding and empathy towards others. You might have a general sense of what your colleagues expect from you and your company, including their goals and needs. However, understanding these accurately is not always straightforward

What if you are making wrong assumptions and have false beliefs, and as a result, your words and actions are not really in line with what your colleagues are thinking and feeling? This is a recipe for ineffective relationships and performance.

Although no one can really argue the value of powerful questions, how often do you pose meaningful questions to your colleagues and teammates? What questions are you asking? Are you using the right terminology? Are you asking too many close-ended questions? And finally, are you using the answers to help strengthen your relationships or help others improve their awareness and performance?

If you are asking questions and not doing anything with the responses, what is the point? It can create the opposite result you are trying to achieve. Asking questions goes far beyond exchanging information.

Here is a quote I find very relevant to asking the right questions:

*"The tough thing is figuring out what questions to ask, but once you do that, the rest is really easy."* Elon Musk.

And, there is no need to come up with counterproductive questions or even spend hours trying to figure out the much-needed powerful questions. I have done all the heavy lifting for you.

This book, "555 Powerful Leadership Coaching Questions" is a culmination of essential questions tailored to the evolving professional landscape, including remote work, digital communication, diverse and multi-generational teams, and various professional challenges and opportunities. It covers a broad spectrum of leadership themes such as Visionary Leadership, Ethical Leadership, Digital Leadership, Crisis Management, Cultural Competency, and many more.

These questions will help you ask the right questions that draw out insightful answers—answers that can help you transform your business and yourself into the leader you want or need to become.

By embracing these questions, you will not only improve your leadership and decision-making but also foster stronger, more meaningful relationships within your organization.

Read the following guidelines to learn more about asking powerful questions that unlock learning, enhance leadership, and improve performance in the modern professional landscape.

- **Effective questions are open or focused, depending on the context:** Questions that open awareness and learning are open-ended questions that cannot be answered with a simple yes or no. These questions evoke deeper thinking and reflection, crucial in today's diverse and multi-generational teams, remote work environments, and digital communication.

- **Effective questions support learning:** Your goal is to stimulate thinking and deepen your colleagues' understanding of the issues at hand. Insightful questions help focus attention on the aspects of the situation that are most valuable, promoting a culture of continuous learning and adaptability.

- **Effective questions are asked for the benefit of others:** The intent of a powerful question is to stimulate your colleagues' thinking and deepen their understanding. It is not about you and what you want, but about facilitating their growth and insights, which is essential in fostering an inclusive and collaborative work environment.

- **Effective questions engage a personal response:** Work is about achieving results, and it is people who create those results. As a leader, your role is to engage colleagues by inviting a personal response—how they feel, what emotions they are bringing to the situation. The more a question invites a personal response, the more powerful it is for facilitating learning and building strong, empathetic relationships.

- **Effective questions look beyond problems to future outcomes:** When a colleague is entangled in a problem, impactful questions shift the perspective from the problem to the solution. This approach opens new opportunities for action and encourages innovative thinking, essential in navigating the complexities of today's professional landscape.
- **Effective questions facilitate openness versus defensiveness:** Impactful questions are worded and expressed with a non-judgmental tone and open body language to prevent defensive reactions. It is usually best to avoid questions that begin with "why," as they can elicit defensive responses or explanations. Instead, focus on what, how, and when to promote open dialogue.
- **Effective questions co-create best options versus manipulating outcomes:** Impactful questions are not intended to manipulate or lead colleagues to the option you might think is best. If you have a suggestion, it is best to make it directly as a suggestion rather than disguising it as a question. This approach fosters a culture of trust and collaboration.
- **Less is more:** For powerful questions, less is usually more. Ask only one question at a time and avoid long-winded, complicated questions. A short, simple question—such as "What is that all about?" or "What will the consequences be?"—pulls the respondent straight to the core of the issue, facilitating clarity and decisive action.

These guidelines are designed to help you master the art of asking powerful questions in leadership, coaching, and mentoring. By incorporating these principles, you can enhance your leadership effectiveness.

## TIPS FOR THE USE OF THIS BOOK

This book is designed to enhance your leadership, coaching, and mentoring practices through the art of powerful questioning. Here are some tips to maximize its effectiveness:

**1. Flexible Categorization:** We have organized the questions into different chapters based on themes relevant to modern leadership. Use this categorization as a reference. Many questions can fit into multiple categories, so feel free to explore different sections to find the most relevant questions for your needs.

**2. The Power of Listening:** The foundation of any meaningful conversation is active listening. Pay attention to the words, emotions, physical expressions, and energy of the person you are engaging with. This attentiveness will help you ask more insightful and impactful questions.

**3. Tailoring Questions:** For better results, customize the questions to fit the specific conversation and the individual you are speaking with. Personalization enhances the relevance and effectiveness of your inquiries.

**4. Combining Questions:** Combine different questions to delve deeper into discussions and generate more profound insights. This approach can help uncover underlying issues and foster a richer dialogue.

**5. Creative Adaptation:** Some questions include a couple of options along with a blank third option to inspire your creativity. Use this flexibility to craft unique questions that are tailored to your specific context.

**6. Follow-Up Questions:** Asking follow-up questions is essential for diving deeper into conversations and uncovering what truly matters. They help clarify responses and explore topics in more detail.

**7. Adapt to Context:** Questions need to be tailored to the specific conversation you are having. Adjust the wording and focus of your questions to suit the context and the individual's preferences.

**8. Use Your Vocabulary:** Adapt the questions to your own vocabulary. This will make the conversation more natural and relatable for both you and the person you are engaging with.

**9. Keep It Simple:** Ask only one question at a time, and avoid long-winded or complicated questions. Simple, direct questions are more likely to yield clear and meaningful responses.

By following these tips, you can effectively use the questions in this book to enhance your leadership, coaching, and mentoring practices. These questions are designed to help you foster stronger relationships, drive performance, and create a positive impact within your organization.

# TABLE OF CONTENTS

## 1. Visionary Leadership

**Guide strategic foresight into creating actionable visions that anticipate future challenges and opportunities.**

1. How will you ensure your strategic vision aligns with (market trends/future opportunities/_____)?

2. What emerging (technologies/industry shifts/_____) do you see as opportunities for innovation within your organization?

3. How can you cultivate a culture that challenges (the status quo/conventional thinking/_____) and encourages expansive thinking?

4. What strategic (partnerships/alliances/_____) can be pivotal in realizing your vision, and how might you initiate these collaborations?

5. How do you ensure your vision remains (relevant/adaptable/_____) in the face of unforeseen (economic/technological/_____) changes?

6. What are the biggest (challenges/risks/_____) your industry will face in the next decade, and how does your vision proactively address these challenges?

7. How can you communicate your vision to (inspire/mobilize/_____) your organization's stakeholders effectively?

8. What mechanisms do you have in place to regularly (review/revise/_____) your vision based on (new data/changes in the market/_____)?

9. How do you balance (short-term obligations/long-term goals/_____) in your strategic planning?

10. What specific (skills/knowledge/_____) do you need to develop to foresee better and capitalize on (future opportunities/trends/_____)?

11. How can your leadership approach incorporate (inclusive decision-making/diverse perspectives/_____) to enhance the richness of your vision?

12. In what ways can (technology/your team/_____) be leveraged to predict better (trends/adaptations/_____) and adapt your business model accordingly?

13. How do you plan to measure the success of your vision, and what (metrics/indicators/_____) will you use to track (progress/impact/_____)?

14. What do you consider to be the most underestimated (trend/technology/_____) that could impact your industry, and how are you preparing to leverage it?

15. How do you engage (younger employees/new team members/_____) and integrate their perspectives into the evolution of your organizational vision?

16. What lessons have you learned from (past visionary leaders/industry pioneers/_____), and how have these insights shaped your approach to leadership?

## 2. Ethical Leadership

**Emphasize integrity and ethical conduct, ensuring decisions align with organizational values and societal norms.**

1. How do you ensure your decisions align with (organizational values/societal expectations/_____)?

2. What measures have you implemented to promote (transparency/accountability/_____) in your leadership practices?

3. How do you address ethical dilemmas when (company interests/personal values/_____) conflict?

4. What strategies do you use to cultivate a culture of (integrity/ethical behavior/_____) within your team?

5. How do you ensure that your leadership decisions reflect (fairness/justice/_____) in diverse situations?

6. What steps do you take to incorporate (stakeholder input/ethical considerations/_____) into your strategic planning process?

7. How do you handle situations where organizational practices may deviate from (industry norms/ethical standards/_____)?

8. In what ways do you educate your team about (ethical leadership/corporate governance/_____) to enhance their understanding and implementation?

9. How do you monitor and evaluate the ethical impact of your decisions on (employees/communities/_____)?

10. What mechanisms have you established to address and rectify ethical misconduct within (your team/the organization/_____)?

11. How do you lead by example in demonstrating (ethical decision-making/personal integrity/_____) to inspire your team?

12. What are the challenges you face in maintaining ethical leadership, and how do you (overcome these/manage them/_____)?

13. How do you engage with external stakeholders to ensure your business practices are perceived as (ethical/socially responsible/_____)?

14. What are your criteria for evaluating the ethical implications of (new projects/business ventures/_____)?

15. How do you balance profitability with ethical considerations in (day-to-day operations/long-term planning/_____)?

16. What initiatives have you introduced to reinforce the importance of (ethical practices/social responsibility/_____) in your organization?

## 3. Inclusive Leadership

**Promote diversity and inclusion, fostering an environment where diverse perspectives are valued and leveraged.**

1. How do you assess and address gaps in (diversity/inclusion/_____) within your team or organization?

2. What strategies do you employ to ensure diverse (team members/stakeholders/_____) feel valued and heard?

3. How do you tailor your leadership style to accommodate different (cultural backgrounds/personal experiences/_____)?

4. What measures have you implemented to promote (equal opportunities/inclusive practices/_____) in recruitment and promotion processes?

5. How do you facilitate conversations about (diversity/equity/_____) that are both productive and respectful?

6. What training or development opportunities do you provide to enhance (cultural competence/diversity awareness/_____) among your leaders and staff?

7. How do you measure the effectiveness of your diversity and inclusion initiatives in terms of (employee satisfaction/business outcomes/_____)?

8. What practices do you have in place to ensure all team members can contribute to and influence (strategic decisions/organizational culture/_____)?

9. How do you handle instances of (discrimination/bias/_____) to reinforce a culture of inclusion and respect?

10. What role do mentorship and sponsorship play in promoting inclusion within your organization, and how are these roles assigned?

11. How do you ensure that inclusion and diversity considerations are embedded in (project planning/leadership development/_____)?

12. What mechanisms are in place to gather feedback on inclusivity issues from (employees/external stakeholders/_____)?

13. How do you celebrate diverse (backgrounds/cultures/_____) within your organization to enhance employee engagement and unity?

14. How do you leverage diverse perspectives to drive (innovation/problem-solving/_____) in your team?

15. How do you support employees in balancing (work-life commitments/cultural practices/_____) to ensure inclusivity in the workplace?

16. What future initiatives do you plan to implement to advance (diversity/inclusion/_____) in your organization?

## 4. Transformational Leadership

**Focus on initiating change by inspiring, engaging, and transforming organizational culture and practices.**

1. How do you identify areas within your organization that most need transformation (in processes/culture/_____)?

2. What specific leadership behaviors do you demonstrate that encourage others to embrace (change/innovation/_____)?

3. How do you maintain your team's motivation during the uncertainty of (organizational changes/market shifts/_____)?

4. What strategies do you use to align (organizational goals/employee behaviors/_____) with your transformational vision?

5. How do you measure the impact of transformational changes within your organization in terms of (employee engagement/business outcomes/_____)?

6. What role does communication play in your transformational leadership approach, and how do you ensure messages are (clear/consistent/_____)?

7. How do you handle resistance to change from (team members/stakeholders/_____), and what methods do you find most effective?

8. What (training/development initiatives/_____) have you implemented to equip your team with the skills needed for transformational change?

9. How do you foster a culture of (risk-taking/continuous improvement/_____) that supports transformational leadership?

10. In what ways do you gather and incorporate feedback from (employees/clients/_____) to guide the transformation process?

11. How do you ensure that transformational initiatives are sustainable and embedded in the organization's (operations/culture/_____)?

12. What mentoring or coaching practices do you engage in to develop future transformational leaders within your organization (through formal programs/informal sessions/_____)?

13. How do you leverage technology to support transformational change in (leadership practices/team collaboration/_____)?

14. What challenges have you faced in leading transformational changes, and how have you adapted your leadership approach (in response to feedback/from lessons learned/_____)?

15. How do you balance (short-term operational needs/long-term transformational goals/_____)?

16. What success stories can you share where your transformational leadership directly resulted in improved (organizational performance/team dynamics/_____)?

## 5. Sustainable Leadership

**Integrate sustainability into corporate strategies to balance profitability with environmental and social responsibilities.**

1. How do you integrate sustainability goals into your (business strategies/corporate planning/_____)?

2. What measures have you implemented to ensure your organization's operations are environmentally (sustainable/responsible/_____)?

3. How do you assess the social impact of your business decisions on (local communities/the wider society/_____)?

4. What strategies do you employ to balance (short-term profitability/long-term environmental sustainability/_____)?

5. How do you promote and incentivize sustainable practices among your (employees/suppliers/_____)?

6. What initiatives have you introduced to reduce the carbon footprint of your (operations/supply chain/_____)?

7. How do you engage stakeholders in discussions about sustainability to ensure (transparency/broad support/_____)?

8. What challenges have you faced in implementing sustainable practices, and how have you (overcome them/adjusted your strategies/_____)?

9. How do you measure the effectiveness of your sustainability initiatives in terms of (environmental impact/cost savings/_____)?

10. What role does innovation play in your approach to sustainability, and how do you foster creative solutions to (environmental challenges/resource management/_____)?

11. How do you stay informed about (emerging sustainability trends/relevant regulations/_____) and integrate this knowledge into your leadership practices?

12. What partnerships have you formed to enhance the sustainability of your business, and how do these collaborations (improve outcomes/expand impact/_____)?

13. How do you ensure that your commitment to (sustainability/corporate social responsibility/_____) is communicated and understood across all levels of your organization?

14. What specific policies have you implemented to ensure ethical sourcing and (reduce waste/increase recycling/_____) within your organization?

15. How do you involve your customers in your sustainability efforts, and what feedback mechanisms are in place to gauge their (responses/engagement/_____)?

16. Looking forward, what are the next big steps for your organization to further deepen its commitment to (sustainable development/social responsibility/_____)?

## 6. Digital Leadership

**Adopt and implement digital technologies to transform traditional business models and processes.**

1. How do you evaluate new digital technologies for their potential impact on your (business operations/customer engagement/_____)?

2. What steps have you taken to ensure your organization remains agile in the face of rapid digital (innovations/changes/_____)?

3. How do you foster a culture that is open to digital transformation and (continuous learning/technology adoption/_____)?

4. What challenges have you faced in integrating digital technologies, and how have you (overcome them/adjusted your strategies/_____)?

5. How do you balance the risks and benefits of implementing cutting-edge digital tools within your (operations/marketing/_____)?

6. What strategies do you use to protect your organization against digital threats and ensure (cybersecurity/data privacy/_____)?

7. How do you measure the success of your digital initiatives in terms of (ROI/customer satisfaction/_____)?

8. What role does (digital literacy/digital evolution/_____) play in your leadership, and how do you promote it across the organization?

9. How have digital tools transformed your leadership style, particularly in the areas of (communication/team management/_____)?

10. What digital trends do you believe will most significantly impact your industry, and how are you preparing to (leverage them/mitigate risks/_____)?

11. How do you ensure that digital adoption enhances rather than detracts from your organizational culture and employee (engagement/well-being/_____)?

12. How do you involve all stakeholders in your digital transformation journey to ensure buy-in and (effective implementation/broad support/_____)?

13. What practices do you have in place to continuously (monitor/improve/_____) the effectiveness of your digital strategies?

14. How do you decide which digital innovations to prioritize based on your strategic goals and the potential to (reduce costs/improve processes/_____)?

15. How do you maintain (customer trust/employee engagement/_____) as your business models evolve with digital technologies?

16. Looking forward, what are your major (opportunities/business goal/_____) for digital leadership, and how do you plan to achieve them?

## 7. Crisis Management

**Develop resilience and strategic thinking to manage and mitigate crisis situations effectively.**

1. How do you gather and analyze (data/learning lessons/_____) during a crisis to make informed decisions?

2. What lessons have you learned from previous crises that have shaped your (strategies/approaches/_____) for current crisis management?

3. How do you ensure (mental health support/emotional resilience/_____) for your team during and after a crisis?

4. In what ways do you debrief and learn from each crisis situation to improve future (response efforts/preparedness efforts/_____)?

5. How do you balance (short-term responses/long-term recovery/_____) with rebuilding efforts during a crisis?

6. What (leadership qualities/skills/_____) do you find most crucial in crisis situations, and how do you cultivate these in yourself and your team?

7. Looking ahead, what are your strategies for strengthening your organization's overall (resilience/crisis management/_____) against future crises?

8. How do you communicate effectively with (stakeholders/employees/_____) during a crisis to maintain transparency and trust?

9. What processes do you have in place to quickly (identify/assess/_____) and respond to emerging crises?

10. How do you ensure that (resources/support/_____) are adequately allocated during a crisis to meet immediate needs?

11. What role does (technology/data/_____) play in enhancing your crisis management capabilities?

12. How do you integrate (feedback/lessons learned/_____) from past crises into your current crisis management plans?

13. What (training/development/_____) initiatives do you offer to prepare your team for effectively handling crises?

14. How do you maintain (morale/motivation/_____) among your team during prolonged crisis situations?

15. How do you engage with (external partners/community resources/_____) to support your crisis management efforts?

16. What measures do you take to ensure continuity of (operations/critical functions/_____) during a crisis?

## 8. Global Leadership

**Manage and navigate across cultural, geographic, and political boundaries, understanding global market dynamics.**

1. How do you stay informed about international market trends and adapt your strategies to (different cultural contexts/global demands/_____)?

2. What methods do you employ to ensure effective communication across (different time zones/cultural barriers/_____)?

3. How do you develop (cultural competence/global awareness/_____) within your leadership team and broader organization?

4. What challenges have you faced in managing a (global workforce/multicultural team/_____), and how have you addressed these challenges?

5. How do you balance global corporate strategies with (local market needs/local regulations/_____)?

6. What role does diversity play in your global leadership approach, and how do you leverage it to enhance (team innovation/competitive edge/_____)?

7. How do you assess and manage political risks when entering new international markets through (risk assessments/strategic partnerships/_____)?

8. What (strategies/negotiation techniques/_____) do you use to build and maintain strong relationships with international stakeholders?

9. How do you ensure alignment and coherence in organizational practices across different (countries/regions/_____) while respecting local nuances?

10. What have been your key learnings from operating in international markets, and how have these influenced your (leadership style/strategic approach/_____)?

11. How do you foster (innovation/collaboration/_____) within your global teams, ensuring that ideas are freely shared and valued?

12. What types of (KPIs/feedback loops/_____) have you established to monitor and evaluate the performance of your global operations?

13. How do you manage compliance with international laws and standards, and what systems do you have in place to ensure (ethical practices/legal adherence/_____)?

14. How do you handle the complexities of cross-border (logistics/operations/_____) in your global strategy?

15. What (leadership qualities/skills/_____) do you find most effective in a global setting, and how do you cultivate these in your leadership development programs?

16. Looking forward, what emerging markets or regions are you focusing on, and what are your strategies for (successful entry/growth/_____)?

## 9. Adaptive Leadership

**Embrace flexibility and responsiveness, allowing leaders to adjust strategies based on evolving circumstances.**

1. How do you stay informed about changes in your industry, and how quickly can you (implement/respond to/_____) these changes?

2. What processes do you have in place to ensure your leadership approach remains flexible to (market shifts/internal challenges/_____)?

3. How do you encourage your team to be proactive about (identifying potential changes/suggesting innovative solutions/_____)?

4. What techniques do you use to assess the need for change in your strategies and how do you (prioritize these changes/measure their impacts/_____)?

5. How do you balance maintaining core organizational values while fostering an adaptive (work culture/strategy/_____)?

6. What tools or technologies do you utilize to enhance your ability to adapt to (new trends/emerging challenges/_____)?

7. How do you ensure that your team is equipped to handle (uncertainty/change/_____) in their day-to-day roles?

8. What strategies do you implement to gather and act on feedback from (employees/customers/_____) quickly and effectively?

9. How do you lead by example in promoting adaptability within your organization (through decision-making/your personal actions/_____)?

10. What (challenges/problems/_____) have you faced in shifting organizational mindsets to embrace adaptability, and how have you overcome them?

11. How do you adjust your leadership style when faced with (crises/sudden changes/_____) in the external environment?

12. What role does risk (management/avoidance/_____) play in your adaptive leadership strategy, and how do you ensure risks are managed effectively?

13. How do you empower your (team/boss/_____) to make decisions that require quick responses without compromising on quality or compliance?

14. How do you leverage cross-functional teams to increase (organizational agility/profits/_____)

15. How do you (assess/integrate/_____) emerging opportunities into your existing strategies without disrupting ongoing operations?

16. Looking ahead, how do you plan to enhance your (leadership/team/_____) to remain responsive to future industry transformations?

## 10. Remote Work Leadership

**Ensure that remote teams are motivated, productive, and effectively managed through virtual platforms.**

1. How do you establish clear communication protocols for your remote team to ensure the effective sharing of (consistent information/best practices/_____)?

2. What strategies do you implement to maintain high (engagement/communication/_____) levels among remote team members?

3. How do you (monitor/support/_____) the productivity of remote employees without micromanaging?

4. What (tools/technologies/_____) have you found most effective in managing your remote teams, and how do you ensure all team members are proficient in using them?

5. How do you handle timezone differences within your remote team to (maximize collaboration/minimize disruptions/_____)?

6. What measures do you take to foster a sense of (community/belonging/_____) among remote team members who may feel isolated?

7. How do you ensure that remote work policies are fair and inclusive, accommodating different (working styles/personal circumstances/_____)?

8. What (opportunities/challenges/_____) have you faced in leading remote teams, and how have you adapted your leadership style to deal with them?

9. How do you provide consistent (feedback/recognition/_____) to remote team members to keep them motivated and informed about their performance?

10. What strategies do you use to ensure the (mental health/well-being/_____) of your remote employees is addressed?

11. How do you (manage/integrate/_____) new remote team members to ensure they quickly become productive and feel part of the team?

12. What role do digital security practices play in your remote leadership, and how do you educate your team on cybersecurity (risks/ protection protocols/_____)?

13. How do you encourage (innovation/creative thinking/_____) within a remote setting, where spontaneous collaboration is less frequent?

14. What key performance indicators do you focus on when assessing the effectiveness of (your remote leadership/the productivity of your team/_____)?

15. How do you balance synchronous and asynchronous communication to (enhance team efficiency/reduce digital fatigue/_____)?

16. Looking ahead, what (improvements/changes/_____) do you plan to implement in your remote leadership practices to better support your team's needs?

## 11. Health and Wellbeing Leadership

**Prioritize the health and overall well-being of employees to enhance engagement and productivity.**

1. How do you assess the (health/well-being/_____) needs of your employees, and how do you tailor your HR policies to meet these needs?

2. What specific initiatives have you implemented to promote mental health (awareness/support/_____) within your organization?

3. How do you measure the effectiveness of your health and well-being programs in terms of (employee satisfaction/productivity/_____)?

4. What (strategies/practices/_____) do you employ to encourage a healthy work-life balance among your employees?

5. How do you ensure that managers and team leaders are adequately trained to recognize and address signs of (stress/burnout/_____) among their team members?

6. What communication channels do you have in place for employees to safely discuss their (well-being/workload/_____) concerns?

7. How do you foster a (culture/company's values/_____) where health and well-being are seen as integral to professional success?

8. What are the most significant challenges you have faced in integrating health and well-being into your (organizational culture/senior management's priorities/_____), and how have you addressed them?

9. How do you promote physical health among your (employees/senior executives/_____) in a predominantly sedentary work environment?

10. What role do wellness (incentives/benefits/_____) play in your overall employee engagement strategy?

11. How do you evaluate the (ROI/cost/_____) of investing in employee health and well-being programs?

12. How do you integrate health and well-being into your leadership (development programs/style/_____)?

13. What (initiatives/action plans/_____) have you introduced to support the nutritional health of your employees?

14. How do you handle the challenges of (supporting/improving/_____) the mental health of remote or distributed team members?

15. What feedback mechanisms do you use to continuously improve the health and well-being (programs/practices/_____) at your organization?

16. Looking forward, what (emerging trends/innovations/_____) in workplace health and well-being are you considering adopting (digital health tools/wellness apps/_____)?

## 12. Mentoring and Developmental Leadership

**Invest in the growth and development of individuals through coaching, mentoring, and providing continuous learning opportunities.**

1. How do you identify potential (leaders/managers/_____) within your organization, and what criteria do you use to select them?

2. What structured (mentoring/coaching/_____) programs do you have in place, and how do you match participants?

3. How do you measure the effectiveness of your (mentoring/coaching/_____) initiatives?

4. What specific (tools/resources/_____) do you provide to support the ongoing development of your employees?

5. How do you ensure that developmental opportunities are accessible to all employees across different (departments/locations/_____)?

6. What strategies do you use to encourage a culture of (continuous learning/self-improvement/_____)

7. How do you (tailor/launch/_____) development programs to meet the diverse needs of your workforce?

8. What (challenges/opportunities/_____) have you encountered in implementing your developmental leadership initiatives, and how have you addressed these?

9. How do you integrate the principles of (developmental leadership/coaching/_____) into your day-to-day management practices?

10. What role does (feedback/mentoring/_____) play in your developmental strategies, and how do you ensure it is constructive and actionable?

11. How do you support employees in applying new (skills/knowledge/_____) to their work?

12. What impact have your (mentoring/development/_____) programs had on employee retention and engagement?

13. How do you encourage senior leaders to actively participate in (mentoring/coaching/_____) others within the organization?

14. What innovative approaches have you introduced to enhance traditional (mentoring/coaching/_____) methods)?

15. How do you ensure the (continuity/enhancement/_____) of development efforts during organizational changes or disruptions?

16. Looking forward, what new (trends/technologies/_____) are you considering incorporating into your developmental leadership programs?

## 13. Strategic Decision-Making

**Combine analytical insights and strategic foresight to make decisions that positively impact the organization's long-term success.**

1. How do you ensure that your strategic decisions align with the (long-term goals/vision/_____) of your organization?

2. What (frameworks/models/_____) do you use to evaluate the potential impacts of major decisions?

3. How do you incorporate (data analytics/your gut feeling/_____) into your decision-making processes?

4. What steps do you take to ensure diverse (perspectives/teams/_____) are considered in strategic decisions?

5. How do you balance risk and (innovation/profits/_____) when making strategic decisions?

6. What (mechanisms/ feedback loops/_____) have you established to monitor the outcomes of strategic decisions and adjust plans as necessary?

7. How do you cultivate a decision-making culture that encourages (team engagement/critical thinking/_____) among your leaders and staff?

8. What (challenges/opportunities/_____) have you faced in implementing strategic decisions, and how have you managed them?

9. How do you prepare your organization to adapt to unexpected (results/crises/_____) from strategic decisions?

10. What role does (customer/employee/_____) feedback play in shaping your strategic decision-making?

11. How do you ensure (transparency/accountability/_____) in decision-making processes within your leadership team?

12. How do you manage (disagreements/conflicts/_____) that arise during strategic decision-making?

13. What recent (strategic decision/mistake/_____) has transformed your organization, and what were the key factors that led to its success?

14. How do you (assess/manage/_____) the ethical implications of your strategic decisions?

15. How do you stay informed about (industry trends/external factors/_____) that may affect strategic decision-making?

16. Looking ahead, what (emerging strategies/methodologies/_____) are you considering to enhance decision-making effectiveness in your organization?

## 14. Change Leadership

**Manage and influence effective change processes, addressing resistance and aligning stakeholders with new directions.**

1. How do you identify the need for change within your organization, and what (indicators/data/_____) help you decide when to initiate change?

2. What steps do you take to ensure all (shareholders/stakeholders/_____) understand and are aligned with the reasons for change?

3. How do you assess the potential impact of proposed changes on different parts of your (organization/company culture/_____)?

4. What strategies do you employ to gather support and buy-in for change initiatives from resistant (team members/shareholders/_____)?

5. How do you manage the communication process during a change to (ensure transparency/maintain trust/_____)

6. What (tools/techniques/_____) do you use to monitor the progress and effectiveness of change implementation?

7. How do you address the (emotional/psychological/_____) impacts of change on employees?

8. What role do leadership styles play in (facilitating/hindering/_____) change within your organization, and how do you adjust your style to promote effective change?

9. How do you ensure that the changes made are (sustainable/embedded/_____) into the organization's culture?

10. What mechanisms do you have in place for (stakeholders/employees/_____) to provide feedback on changes, and how do you incorporate this feedback into ongoing adjustments?

11. How do you build and maintain momentum for a change initiative when (progress slows/challenges arise/_____)?

12. What (training/development initiatives/_____) do you offer to equip employees with the skills needed to adapt to change?

13. How do you balance the (pace of change/workload/_____) to avoid overwhelming your team while ensuring timely achievement of objectives?

14. What has been your most (challenging/rewarding/_____) change initiative, and what lessons did you learn from it that have shaped your approach to change leadership?

15. How do you leverage (technology/external consultants/_____) to support change processes, particularly in tracking and managing the implementation across various departments?

16. Looking forward, what (emerging trends/tools/_____) are you considering to enhance your change leadership practices?

## 15. Collaborative Leadership

**Cultivate a culture of teamwork and cooperation, breaking down silos and fostering cross-functional collaborations.**

1. How do you define (successful/unsuccessful/_____) collaboration within your organization, and what key indicators do you use to measure its effectiveness?

2. What (strategies/approaches/_____) do you implement to ensure that teams from different departments work together effectively?

3. How do you (address/avoid/_____) conflicts that arise from cross-functional collaborations?

4. What (tools/technologies/_____) do you utilize to facilitate communication and collaboration across different locations and teams?

5. How do you encourage team members to share (knowledge/best practices/_____) across organizational boundaries?

6. What (incentives/recognition/_____) programs do you have in place to reward collaborative efforts and team achievements?

7. How do you ensure that (collaboration/competitiveness/_____) does not compromise individual accountability?

8. What (challenges/opportunities/_____) have you faced in fostering a collaborative environment, and how have you manage them?

9. How do you integrate (new employees/closed minded employees/_____) into existing collaborative frameworks to ensure they quickly become contributing team members?

10. What role do (senior leaders/unit managers/_____) play in modelling collaborative behavior, and how is this monitored and encouraged?

11. How do you balance the need for (collaboration/competitiveness/_____) with the need for efficient decision-making?

12. What (practices/rules/_____) do you have in place to ensure continuous improvement in your collaborative processes?

13. How do you tailor collaboration strategies to fit the diverse (working styles/cultural backgrounds/_____) of your team members?

14. What (feedback mechanisms/questions/_____) do you use to gather insights on the effectiveness of your collaborative leadership?

15. How do you use (data/analytics/_____) to track the progress and impact of collaborative projects?

16. Looking forward, what emerging (trends/tools/_____) are you considering to enhance collaboration within your organization?

## 16. Resilient Leadership

**Demonstrate the capacity to recover quickly from difficulties, maintaining steadfast leadership amidst challenges.**

1. How do you assess and enhance your personal resilience as a (leader/team member/_____)?

2. What strategies do you employ to maintain your (focus/drive/_____) during times of uncertainty or stress?

3. How do you support your team's resilience during (organizational challenges/organizational growth periods/_____)?

4. What lessons have you learned from past failures, and how have you applied these lessons to strengthen your (leadership resilience/team's leadership resilience/_____)?

5. How do you manage to balance short-term crisis management with long-term strategic goals during (tough times/growth periods/_____)?

6. What (tools/resources/_____) do you find most effective in building resilience within your team?

7. How do you ensure (effective decision-making/having a clear mind/_____) under pressure, and what techniques help you maintain clarity and calm?

8. What mechanisms do you have in place to monitor the well-being of your staff during (high-pressure/recession/_____) periods?

9. How do you foster a culture of (open communication/mutual support/_____) in your team, particularly during crises?

10. What role does (leadership visibility/coaching/_____) play in your approach to resilient leadership, and how do you maintain your presence during critical periods?

11. How do you (encourage/reward/_____) expressions of resilience and innovative problem-solving among your team members?

12. What practices do you follow to ensure your own (mental/physical/_____) well-being as a leader, which in turn supports your ability to lead effectively?

13. How do you deal with the emotional impact of tough leadership decisions on (yourself/your team/_____)?

14. In what ways do you utilize (setbacks/challenges/_____) as opportunities for leadership growth and organizational learning?

15. How do you maintain trust and confidence among (stakeholders/employees/_____) during times of change or adversity?

16. Looking ahead, what steps are you taking to further develop your (resilience/team's resilience/_____) and that of your organization to prepare for future challenges?

## 17. Empathetic Leadership

**Employ empathy to connect with and understand the needs and motivations of others, enhancing interpersonal relationships.**

1. How do you actively practice empathy in your (day-to-day leadership interactions/performance reviews/_____)?

2. What specific strategies do you employ to understand the diverse (personal/professional/_____) backgrounds of your team members?

3. How do you ensure that your leadership decisions consider the (emotional/psychological/_____) impacts on your employees?

4. What techniques do you use to (build trust/create a safe space/_____) for employees to express their concerns and challenges?

5. How do you balance organizational goals with the (personal/professional/_____) needs of your team members?

6. In what ways do you demonstrate (understanding/support/_____) for team members going through personal challenges?

7. How do you facilitate empathy among your (team members/senior executives/_____), encouraging them to support each other?

8. What (challenges/opportunities/_____) have you faced when trying to lead empathetically, and how have you managed them?

9. How do you measure the effectiveness of your empathetic leadership in enhancing team (cohesion/productivity/_____)?

10. What role does empathy play in your (conflict resolution/communication/_____) strategies, and how has it affected the outcomes?

11. How do you incorporate empathy into your leadership development programs for (employees/other leaders/_____) within your organization?

12. How do you ensure that your approach to empathetic leadership is perceived as genuine and not merely a leadership tactic (consistency/authentic actions/_____)?

13. What feedback mechanisms do you have in place to assess how your empathetic actions are received by your (team/senior leadership team/_____)?

14. How do you handle situations where empathy might conflict with making tough decisions for the (organization/shareholders/_____)?

15. How do you maintain your own emotional health while being an empathetic (leader/colleague/_____)?

16. Looking forward, how do you plan to further develop your empathetic leadership skills to meet the evolving needs of your (organization/stakeholders/_____)?

## 18. Accountable Leadership

**Hold oneself and others accountable for actions and decisions, fostering a culture of transparency and trust.**

1. How do you define accountability within your leadership role, and what measures do you take to model this behavior to your (team/junior employees/_____)?

2. What systems do you have in place to ensure that all team members understand their (responsibilities/goals/_____) placed upon them?

3. How do you handle situations where (team members/business owners/_____) fail to meet their commitments, and what processes are in place to address these failures?

4. What (strategies/protocols/_____) do you employ to create a transparent work environment where decisions and processes are open to scrutiny by all stakeholders?

5. How do you ensure that accountability is maintained without creating a culture of (blame/fear/_____) among your team members?

6. What (tools/technologies/_____) do you use to track and measure the performance and accountability of your team?

7. How do you balance the need for accountability with the need to maintain a (supportive/encouraging/_____) work atmosphere?

8. What role does feedback play in your accountability framework, and how do you ensure that it is (constructive/continuous/_____)?

9. How do you involve your team in setting their own (goals/accountability standards/_____) to increase their engagement and ownership of outcomes?

10. What measures do you take to ensure that accountability extends to (ethical practices/adherence to organizational values/_____)?

11. How do you address accountability in (remote/hybrid/_____) work settings, ensuring that distance does not dilute responsibility and transparency?

12. What (training/development initiatives/_____) do you provide to enhance understanding and implementation of accountability across the organization?

13. How do you celebrate instances of strong (accountability/responsibility/_____) taken by team members, reinforcing the positive aspects of this culture?

14. How do you ensure that (leaders/employees/_____) at all levels of your organization are held accountable, creating a uniform standard of accountability?

15. What challenges have you faced in instilling a culture of (accountability/responsibility/_____), and how have you overcome these challenges?

16. Looking forward, how do you plan to further enhance (accountability/responsibility/_____) within your leadership and across the organization to adapt to changing business landscapes?

## 19. Innovative Leadership

**Encourage a culture of innovation where creative ideas and novel approaches are actively pursued and valued.**

1. How do you define innovation within your (leadership/organizational/_____) context?

2. What specific strategies do you employ to encourage (creative thinking/innovation/_____) among your team members?

3. How do you create a safe environment where employees feel free to (experiment/take risks/_____) without fear of failure?

4. What mechanisms are in place to ensure that innovative ideas are (captured/evaluated/_____) effectively?

5. How do you balance the need for ongoing operations with the need to pursue (new/innovative/_____) projects?

6. What (resources/tools/_____) do you allocate specifically for innovation and research and development activities?

7. How do you encourage collaboration across different (departments/leaders/_____) to foster innovation and how is cross-functional teamwork facilitated?

8. What are some of the most significant innovations that have emerged under your leadership and what impact have they had on your (organization/stakeholders/_____)?

9. How do you measure the success of your (innovation initiatives/creative-thinking training programs/_____) and what metrics or KPIs do you use?

10. What challenges have you encountered in trying to embed an innovative culture within your (organization/leadership team/_____), and how have you addressed these challenges?

11. How do you stay informed about (industry trends/technological advancements/_____) to guide the innovation strategy within your organization?

12. How do you ensure that your innovation efforts align with the (strategic goals/values/_____) of your organization?

13. What role does (customer feedback/employee feedback/_____) play in shaping your innovation processes and how do you integrate their insights into new developments?

14. How do you (lead/manage/_____) change that comes as a result of implementing new ideas and innovations within your team or organization?

15. How do you cultivate a mindset of (continuous improvement/lifelong learning/_____) within your organization to support ongoing innovation?

16. Looking forward, what (emerging technologies/ideas/_____) are you considering incorporating into your leadership practice to enhance innovation further?

## 20. Communication Leadership

**Master effective communication strategies to clearly convey messages and engage with various stakeholders.**

1. How do you tailor your communication style to effectively address different (audiences/cultures/_____) within your organization?

2. What strategies do you use to (ensure clarity/avoid misunderstandings/_____) in your communications?

3. How do you measure the effectiveness of your communication efforts within your (team/broader organization/_____)?

4. What role does storytelling play in your leadership communications, and how do you use it to (engage/inspire/_____) your team?

5. How do you handle communications (during a crisis/when delivering difficult news/_____) to your team or stakeholders?

6. What (tools/platforms/_____) do you find most effective for reaching all members of your organization, and how do you ensure messages are received and understood?

7. How do you gather feedback on your communication (style/effectiveness/_____), and how do you incorporate this feedback into your practice?

8. What methods do you use to encourage (open communication/dialogue/_____) within your team?

9. How do you ensure that your non-verbal communication aligns with and supports your (verbal messaging/values/_____)?

10. How do you (train/support/_____) your managers or team leaders in developing their communication skills?

11. What specific communication challenges have you faced while leading (diverse/remote/_____) teams, and how have you addressed them?

12. How do you leverage digital tools to enhance (communication/collaboration/_____) across your organization?

13. How do you balance transparency and the need for (discretion/privacy/_____) in your communications?

14. What practices do you follow to stay consistent in your communications across all levels of the (organization/management/_____)?

15. How do you ensure that important messages are (reinforced/remembered/_____) throughout the organization?

16. Looking forward, what emerging (communication trends/technologies/_____) are you considering adopting to enhance your leadership communication strategies?

## 21. Technological Fluency

**Keep abreast of emerging technologies to enhance organizational competitiveness and operational efficiency.**

1. How do you stay informed about the latest (technological advancements/industry innovations/_____) relevant to your industry?

2. What criteria do you use to evaluate which (new technologies/digital tools/_____) to adopt within your organization?

3. How do you assess the potential impact of implementing (new technologies/advanced systems/_____) on your organization's operational efficiency?

4. What strategies do you employ to foster a culture of (technological adaptation/innovation/_____) among your team members?

5. How do you balance the investment in (new technology/modern systems/_____) with the expected ROI for these tools and systems?

6. What training programs do you implement to ensure your staff is proficient in using (new technologies/digital tools/_____)?

7. How do you manage the challenges associated with replacing (legacy systems/old infrastructure/_____) with new technological solutions?

8. What measures do you take to ensure (data security/privacy protection/_____) when adopting new digital tools and platforms?

9. How do you involve different stakeholders in decisions related to (technological investments/implementations/_____)?

10. What role does technology play in your (decision-making processes/strategic planning/_____), and how has it changed the way your leadership team operates?

11. How do you ensure that the adoption of (new technologies/digital innovations/_____) aligns with your organization's core values and mission?

12. What are the biggest barriers to (technological adoption/digital transformation/_____) in your organization, and how do you overcome these obstacles?

13. How do you track and measure the effectiveness of (new technologies/advanced systems/_____) in enhancing productivity and competitiveness?

14. What success stories can you share where (technological integration/digital transformation/_____) has significantly benefited your organization?

15. How do you handle resistance or skepticism from employees towards (new technology/digital tools/_____), and how do you motivate them to embrace change?

16. Looking ahead, what emerging technologies are you most excited about, and how do you plan to integrate them into your (strategic planning/future projects/_____)?

## 22. Emotional Intelligence

**Manage emotions intelligently to enhance personal performance and the development of strong leadership relationships.**

1. How do you recognize and regulate your emotions in (stressful situations/remote work environments/_____) to maintain effective leadership?

2. What strategies do you use to develop empathy and understanding for (diverse team members/multi-generational teams/_____) in your organization?

3. How do you manage emotional responses during (virtual meetings/digital communications/_____) to ensure clear and effective communication?

4. What methods do you employ to build strong emotional connections with your team, particularly in (remote work settings/virtual environments/_____)?

5. How do you handle emotional triggers that may arise from (workplace conflicts/professional challenges/_____) and maintain composure?

6. What techniques do you use to enhance self-awareness and understand how your emotions impact (decision-making/leadership effectiveness/_____)?

7. How do you foster a culture of emotional intelligence within (diverse teams/remote teams/_____) to improve collaboration and trust?

8. What role does emotional intelligence play in your approach to (conflict resolution/team dynamics/_____), and how do you apply it?

9. How do you provide emotional support to team members facing (personal challenges/professional stress/_____) while maintaining professional boundaries?

10. What practices do you follow to continuously improve your emotional intelligence, such as (self-reflection/feedback/_____)?

11. How do you balance showing empathy with maintaining (authority/accountability/_____) in leadership situations?

12. In what ways do you use emotional intelligence to navigate (cultural differences/communication barriers/_____) in your team?

13. How do you encourage and develop emotional intelligence skills among (your leadership team/your employees/_____)?

14. What impact has improving your emotional intelligence had on your (professional relationships/personal performance/_____)?

15. How do you adapt your emotional intelligence strategies to meet the needs of (remote team members/younger employees/_____) in a changing work environment?

16. Looking ahead, what steps will you take to further integrate emotional intelligence into your (leadership development programs/organizational culture/_____)?

## 23. Cross-Generational Leadership

**Skillfully manages and motivates a diverse age group within the workforce, understanding and respecting generational differences.**

1. How do you tailor your communication strategies to effectively engage (different generations/age groups/_____) within your team?

2. What approaches do you use to understand and address the unique motivations of (younger employees/older employees/_____)?

3. How do you create an inclusive work environment that respects and values (generational differences/diverse perspectives/_____)?

4. What methods do you employ to foster collaboration between (multi-generational team members/cross-age group teams/_____)?

5. How do you handle conflicts that arise from (generational misunderstandings/differing work styles/_____) within your workforce?

6. What strategies do you use to leverage the strengths of (each generation/different age groups/_____) to enhance team performance?

7. How do you adapt your leadership style to meet the needs of (diverse age groups/multi-generational teams/_____)?

8. What initiatives do you implement to encourage mentorship and knowledge sharing between (younger employees/experienced employees/_____)?

9. How do you address the expectations of (different generations/multi-generational team members/_____) in a remote work environment?

10. What training programs do you offer to develop cross-generational understanding and respect among (team members/leaders/_____)?

11. How do you ensure that (digital communication tools/virtual platforms/_____) are accessible and user-friendly for all age groups?

12. What practices do you follow to balance the varying career aspirations and goals of (different generations/diverse age groups/_____) within your team?

13. How do you recognize and celebrate the contributions of (each generation/different age groups/_____) to foster a sense of belonging and appreciation?

14. What challenges have you faced in leading a multi-generational team, and how have you adapted your (leadership style/strategies/_____) to overcome them?

15. How do you encourage continuous learning and development for (all age groups/different generations/_____) in your organization?

16. Looking ahead, what steps will you take to further enhance cross-generational leadership practices and ensure (cohesion/integration/_____) within your workforce?

## 24. Purpose-Driven Leadership

**Aligns organizational objectives with a clear purpose, enhancing employee motivation and societal impact.**

1. How do you define and communicate the core purpose of your organization to (employees/stakeholders/_____)?

2. What strategies do you use to align your team's daily activities with the organization's (core values/mission/_____)?

3. How do you measure the impact of your organization's purpose on (employee motivation/societal impact/_____)?

4. How do you integrate purpose-driven goals into your (strategic planning/performance metrics/_____)?

5. What initiatives do you implement to ensure that all employees understand and embrace the organization's (purpose/mission/_____)?

6. How do you foster a culture that prioritizes (purpose-driven work/social impact/_____) among your team members?

7. What role does digital communication play in spreading and reinforcing your organization's (purpose/core values/_____)?

8. How do you adapt your leadership approach to inspire purpose-driven work in (remote teams/multi-generational teams/_____)?

9. How do you handle conflicts between short-term business goals and the long-term purpose of your organization (balancing priorities/strategic adjustments/_____)?

10. What methods do you use to gather feedback on how well your organization's purpose is understood and implemented by (employees/stakeholders/_____)?

11. How do you recognize and reward employees who exemplify the organization's (purpose/values/_____) in their work?

12. What strategies do you use to integrate the organization's purpose into (hiring practices/onboarding programs/_____)?

13. How do you ensure that your organization's purpose remains relevant and impactful in (changing market conditions/evolving societal expectations/_____)?

14. What practices do you follow to align your leadership decisions with the organization's (core purpose/mission/_____)?

15. How do you engage with external stakeholders to amplify the societal impact of your organization's (purpose-driven initiatives/community programs/_____)?

16. Looking ahead, what steps will you take to further embed purpose-driven leadership into your (strategic goals/organizational culture/_____)?

## 25. Data-Driven Decision Making

**Leverages data analytics to inform and enhance decision-making processes, improving accuracy and outcomes.**

1. How do you ensure that your team has access to accurate and relevant (data sources/analytics tools/_____) to support decision-making?

2. What criteria do you use to evaluate the reliability and validity of (data sets/analytical methods/_____) used in your decision-making processes?

3. How do you integrate data analytics into your (strategic planning/performance evaluation/_____) to enhance decision-making?

4. What strategies do you employ to foster a culture that values (data-driven insights/evidence-based decisions/_____) among your team members?

5. How do you balance the use of data analytics with (intuitive judgment/experience-based insights/_____) in your leadership approach?

6. What training programs do you implement to ensure your staff is proficient in (data analysis/interpretation/_____)?

7. How do you handle challenges related to (data privacy/data security/_____) while leveraging data analytics in decision-making?

8. What measures do you take to ensure that data-driven decisions are aligned with your organization's (values/strategic goals/_____)?

9. How do you involve different stakeholders in the (data collection/analysis/_____) process to ensure comprehensive insights?

10. What role does technology play in enhancing your (data analytics capabilities/decision-making processes/_____), and how has it changed your approach to leadership?

11. How do you ensure that the adoption of data analytics tools aligns with your organization's (core values/mission/_____)?

12. What are the biggest (barriers/opportunities/_____) to implementing data-driven decision-making in your organization, and how do you overcome them?

13. How do you track and measure the effectiveness of data-driven decisions in enhancing (organizational performance/operational efficiency/_____)?

14. What (success stories/learning lessons/_____) can you share where data-driven decision-making has significantly benefited your organization?

15. How do you address resistance or skepticism from employees towards data analytics, and how do you motivate them to embrace (data-driven approaches/new technologies/_____)?

16. Looking ahead, what steps will you take to further integrate data analytics into your (strategic planning/leadership practices/_____)?

## 26. Agile Leadership

**Implement agile practices across the organization to enhance flexibility, responsiveness, and innovation.**

1. How do you foster a culture of (flexibility/adaptability/_____) within your organization to support agile practices?

2. What strategies do you use to implement agile methodologies in (remote teams/multi-generational teams/_____) to enhance collaboration?

3. How do you ensure that your leadership style aligns with the principles of (agility/responsiveness/_____)?

4. What measures do you take to encourage continuous (innovation/improvement/_____) among your team members?

5. How do you balance the need for (structure/processes/_____) with the need for agility and rapid response to changes?

6. What (training programs/courses/_____) do you offer to develop agile skills within your team?

7. How do you manage resistance to agile practices from employees who are accustomed to (traditional methods/hierarchical structures/_____)?

8. What tools and technologies do you leverage to support (agile workflows/collaborative environments/_____)?

9. How do you measure the success of agile implementations in terms of (team performance/innovation outcomes/_____)?

10. What role does (communication/feedback/_____) play in maintaining agile practices across your organization?

11. How do you ensure that agile practices are consistently applied across (different departments/teams/_____)?

12. What are the biggest challenges you face in maintaining agility in (remote work environments/digital communication/_____), and how do you overcome them?

13. How do you integrate agile principles into your (strategic planning/decision-making/_____) processes?

14. What success stories can you share where agile practices have significantly improved (organizational flexibility/response times/_____)?

15. How do you promote a mindset of (experimentation/learning from failure/_____) within your agile teams?

16. Looking ahead, what steps will you take to further embed agile practices into your (organizational culture/leadership approach/_____)?

## 27. Entrepreneurial Leadership

**Foster an entrepreneurial spirit within the organization, encouraging risk-taking and proactive problem-solving.**

1. How do you cultivate an entrepreneurial mindset among your team members, encouraging (risk-taking/proactive problem-solving/_____)?

2. What strategies do you use to support and reward (innovative ideas/entrepreneurial initiatives/_____) within your organization?

3. How do you balance the need for (stability/structure/_____) with fostering a culture of entrepreneurship?

4. What measures do you take to create a safe environment for (experimentation/failure/_____) without fear of repercussions?

5. How do you leverage (digital communication tools/remote work environments/_____) to enhance entrepreneurial thinking in your team?

6. What training programs do you offer to develop (entrepreneurial skills/creative thinking/_____) among your employees?

7. How do you encourage (cross-functional collaboration/interdisciplinary projects/_____) to drive entrepreneurial initiatives?

8. What role does (mentorship/coaching/_____) play in fostering an entrepreneurial culture within your organization?

9. How do you handle resistance from (employees/stakeholders/_____) who are hesitant to adopt an entrepreneurial approach?

10. What tools and technologies do you utilize to support (entrepreneurial projects/innovative solutions/_____) within your organization?

11. How do you integrate entrepreneurial thinking into your (strategic planning/decision-making/_____) processes?

12. What are the biggest challenges you face in maintaining an entrepreneurial culture in (remote work settings/diverse teams/_____), and how do you overcome them?

13. How do you measure the impact of entrepreneurial initiatives on (organizational growth/performance/_____)?

14. What success stories can you share where entrepreneurial leadership has led to significant (innovations/business growth/_____) within your organization?

15. How do you promote continuous learning and development in (entrepreneurship/innovation/_____) among your team members?

16. Looking ahead, what steps will you take to further embed entrepreneurial leadership into your (organizational culture/leadership approach/_____)?

## 28. Networked Leadership

**Build and maintain strategic networks both within and outside the organization to enhance influence and knowledge exchange.**

1. How do you identify and cultivate strategic networks within (your organization/your industry/_____) to enhance your influence?

2. What strategies do you use to maintain strong relationships with (internal stakeholders/external partners/_____)?

3. How do you leverage digital communication tools to build and sustain (professional networks/knowledge exchange/_____)?

4. What methods do you employ to encourage (cross-functional collaboration/interdepartmental networking/_____) within your organization?

5. How do you balance the time and effort spent on (network building/relationship maintenance/_____) with your other leadership responsibilities?

6. What training programs do you offer to develop (networking skills/relationship-building abilities/_____) among your team members?

7. How do you handle challenges in maintaining relationships with (remote colleagues/virtual teams/_____)?

8. What role do (mentorship/coaching/_____) programs play in fostering a culture of networked leadership within your organization?

9. How do you measure the effectiveness of your strategic networks in terms of (knowledge exchange/influence/_____)?

10. What tools and technologies do you use to facilitate (network building/information sharing/_____) within and outside your organization?

11. How do you integrate networked leadership into your (strategic planning/decision-making/_____) processes?

12. What are the biggest challenges you face in building and maintaining strategic networks in (remote work environments/diverse teams/_____), and how do you overcome them?

13. How do you encourage your team members to actively participate in (professional networks/industry associations/_____)?

14. What success stories can you share where networked leadership has led to significant (innovations/business opportunities/_____) for your organization?

15. How do you promote continuous learning and development in (networking/relationship building/_____) among your team members?

16. Looking ahead, what steps will you take to further enhance your networked leadership practices to ensure (greater influence/effective knowledge exchange/_____)?

## 29. Cultural Competency

**Understand and adapt to cultural differences, facilitating effective communication and interaction in diverse environments.**

1. How do you assess and improve your understanding of (cultural differences/diverse backgrounds/_____) within your team?

2. What strategies do you use to facilitate effective communication in (multicultural teams/remote environments/_____)?

3. How do you integrate cultural competency into your (leadership practices/team interactions/_____)?

4. What methods do you employ to ensure that your organization's values respect and embrace (cultural diversity/inclusivity/_____)?

5. How do you address and resolve conflicts that arise from (cultural misunderstandings/differences in cultural norms/_____)?

6. What training programs do you offer to develop (cultural awareness/cultural sensitivity/_____) among your employees?

7. How do you adapt your communication style to meet the needs of (diverse team members/international colleagues/_____)?

8. What role does (cultural empathy/intercultural communication/_____) play in your leadership approach?

9. How do you handle challenges related to (language barriers/different communication styles/_____) in a multicultural team?

10. What initiatives do you implement to promote (cultural exchange/inclusive practices/_____) within your organization?

11. How do you measure the effectiveness of your cultural competency initiatives in (enhancing team performance/fostering inclusivity/_____)?

12. What success stories can you share where cultural competency has significantly improved (team collaboration/business outcomes/_____) in your organization?

13. How do you encourage continuous learning and development in (cultural competency/diversity and inclusion/_____) among your team members?

14. How do you integrate cultural competency into your (strategic planning/organizational policies/_____)?

15. What are the biggest challenges you face in fostering cultural competency in (remote teams/multi-generational teams/_____), and how do you overcome them?

16. Looking ahead, what steps will you take to further enhance cultural competency within your (leadership approach/organizational culture/_____)?

## 30. Holistic Health Leadership

**Advocate for a balanced approach to physical, mental, and social well-being in the workplace.**

1. How do you (assess/promote/_____) physical well-being among your team members in the workplace?

2. What strategies do you implement to (support mental health/reduce stress/_____) for employees?

3. How do you foster (social well-being/sense of community/_____) in a remote or hybrid work environment?

4. What role does holistic health play in your leadership approach to (enhancing productivity/improving morale/_____)?

5. How do you ensure that your organization's policies support a balanced approach to (work-life integration/employee well-being/_____)?

6. What measures do you take to address the well-being needs of (multi-generational teams/diverse workforces/_____) in your organization?

7. How do you encourage employees to take personal responsibility for their (physical health/mental well-being/_____)?

8. What training programs do you offer to raise awareness and educate employees about (holistic health/self-care practices/_____)?

9. How do you handle challenges related to maintaining holistic health practices in (high-stress environments/remote work settings/_____)?

10. What initiatives do you implement to ensure a supportive environment for (mental health/social well-being/_____) among team members?

11. How do you measure the impact of holistic health programs on (employee engagement/organizational performance/_____)?

12. What success stories can you share where holistic health leadership has significantly benefited (employee retention/team cohesion/_____) in your organization?

13. How do you integrate holistic health principles into your (strategic planning/leadership development/_____) processes?

14. What role does digital technology play in promoting (holistic health/well-being initiatives/_____) within your team?

15. How do you ensure that remote employees feel supported in their (physical well-being/mental health/_____) despite the lack of in-person interaction?

16. Looking ahead, what steps will you take to further enhance holistic health practices within your (leadership approach/organizational culture/_____)?

## 31. Eco-Leadership

**Champion environmental stewardship, integrating eco-friendly practices into business operations and culture.**

1. How do you incorporate (environmental sustainability/eco-friendly practices/_____) into your organization's core values and mission?

2. What strategies do you use to promote (green initiatives/sustainable practices/_____) among your team members?

3. How do you measure the impact of your eco-leadership initiatives on (business operations/environmental footprint/_____)?

4. What training programs do you offer to educate employees about (environmental stewardship/sustainable practices/_____)?

5. How do you encourage remote and on-site employees to adopt (eco-friendly behaviors/sustainable habits/_____) in their daily work routines?

6. What role does digital communication play in promoting (environmental awareness/green initiatives/_____) within your organization?

7. How do you handle challenges related to implementing (eco-friendly practices/sustainability initiatives/_____) across different departments?

8. What measures do you take to ensure that your supply chain adheres to (sustainable practices/environmental standards/_____)?

9. How do you integrate environmental considerations into your (strategic planning/business decisions/_____)?

10. What role does (innovation/technology/_____) play in advancing your organization's eco-leadership goals?

11. How do you engage with stakeholders to support and enhance your (environmental initiatives/sustainability efforts/_____)?

12. What success stories can you share where eco-leadership has significantly improved your (company's reputation/operational efficiency/_____)?

13. How do you balance the need for (business growth/profitability/_____) with your commitment to environmental stewardship?

14. What initiatives do you implement to reduce your organization's (carbon footprint/waste production/_____)?

15. How do you foster a culture of continuous improvement in (environmental sustainability/eco-friendly practices/_____) among your team members?

16. Looking ahead, what steps will you take to further integrate eco-leadership into your (organizational culture/leadership approach/_____)?

## 32. Privacy and Cybersecurity Leadership

**Prioritize data privacy and cybersecurity, safeguarding organizational and customer data from breaches.**

1. How do you assess and prioritize the (privacy/cybersecurity/_____) needs of your organization to safeguard data effectively?

2. What strategies do you implement to ensure that your team follows best practices in (data privacy/cybersecurity/_____)?

3. How do you stay informed about the latest (cybersecurity threats/privacy regulations/_____) to protect organizational and customer data?

4. What training programs do you offer to educate employees about (cybersecurity risks/data privacy/_____)?

5. How do you handle challenges related to (remote work/digital communication/_____) while maintaining robust cybersecurity measures?

6. What role does technology play in enhancing your organization's (data protection/cybersecurity/_____) efforts?

7. How do you ensure that your organization complies with (privacy laws/cybersecurity standards/_____) across different regions and markets?

8. What measures do you take to protect your organization against (data breaches/cyber attacks/_____)?

9. How do you integrate (privacy considerations/cybersecurity measures/_____) into your strategic planning and decision-making processes?

10. What tools and technologies do you use to monitor and respond to (cyber threats/data breaches/_____) in real-time?

11. How do you foster a culture of (cybersecurity awareness/data privacy/_____) within your team?

12. What initiatives do you implement to ensure that customer data is protected and that (privacy policies/security protocols/_____) are transparent and effective?

13. How do you manage the risks associated with (third-party vendors/supply chain partners/_____) to ensure they adhere to your cybersecurity standards?

14. What success stories can you share where your privacy and cybersecurity leadership has prevented (data breaches/cyber attacks/_____) or minimized their impact?

15. How do you balance the need for (innovation/business agility/_____) with the need to maintain stringent cybersecurity measures?

16. Looking ahead, what steps will you take to further enhance your organization's (cybersecurity/data privacy/_____) practices to stay ahead of emerging threats?

## 33. Human-Centric Leadership

**Place a high value on human capital, ensuring that technology and processes enhance, not replace, human work.**

1. How do you ensure that (technology/processes/_____) enhance the work of your team members rather than replace it?

2. What strategies do you use to maintain a balance between (automation/human input/_____) in your organization?

3. How do you involve your team in decisions regarding the implementation of new (technologies/processes/_____) to ensure their needs are met?

4. What measures do you take to promote the value of (human skills/creativity/_____) in a technologically advanced workplace?

5. How do you ensure that remote work arrangements do not diminish the (human connection/team collaboration/_____) within your organization?

6. What training programs do you offer to help employees adapt to new (technologies/work processes/_____) while enhancing their existing skills?

7. How do you foster a culture that values (human interaction/relationship building/_____) in a digital work environment?

8. What role does (emotional intelligence/empathetic leadership/_____) play in your human-centric leadership approach?

9. How do you address concerns from employees who feel that (technology/automation/_____) might threaten their jobs?

10. What initiatives do you implement to ensure that (technological advancements/process improvements/_____) benefit all employees?

11. How do you integrate human-centric principles into your (strategic planning/business decisions/_____)?

12. What success stories can you share where human-centric leadership has significantly improved (employee satisfaction/organizational performance/_____)?

13. How do you measure the impact of human-centric practices on (employee engagement/productivity/_____)?

14. What tools and technologies do you use to support (human-centric initiatives/employee well-being/_____) in your organization?

15. How do you ensure that diverse and multi-generational teams feel valued and included in a (technology-driven workplace/remote environment/_____)?

16. Looking ahead, what steps will you take to further embed human-centric leadership into your (organizational culture/leadership approach/_____)?

## 34. Leadership Branding

**Develop a distinctive leadership brand that resonates with stakeholders and aligns with organizational values.**

1. How do you define your leadership brand, and what (core values/unique qualities/_____) does it embody?

2. What strategies do you use to ensure your leadership brand aligns with your organization's (mission/values/_____)?

3. How do you communicate your leadership brand to (employees/stakeholders/_____) effectively?

4. What measures do you take to maintain consistency in your leadership brand across (different platforms/various communication channels/_____)?

5. How do you incorporate feedback from (team members/colleagues/_____) to refine and strengthen your leadership brand?

6. What role does digital communication play in shaping and promoting your leadership brand (online presence/social media/_____)?

7. How do you ensure your leadership brand resonates with a (diverse audience/multi-generational team/_____)?

8. What initiatives do you implement to demonstrate your leadership brand in (daily interactions/strategic decisions/_____)?

9. How do you balance (authenticity/openness/_____) with strategic image-building in your leadership branding efforts?

10. What steps do you take to align your personal leadership brand with your organization's (brand identity/corporate culture/_____)?

11. How do you measure the impact of your leadership brand on (employee engagement/stakeholder trust/_____)?

12. What success stories can you share where a strong leadership brand has led to significant (organizational success/positive change/_____)?

13. How do you adapt your leadership brand to remain relevant in (changing market conditions/evolving professional landscapes/_____)?

14. What (tools/technologies/_____) do you use to enhance and promote your leadership?

15. How do you (mentor/develop/_____) future leaders to cultivate their own leadership?

16. Looking ahead, what steps will you take to further evolve and enhance your leadership brand to meet (future challenges/stakeholder expectations/_____)?

## 35. Social Impact Leadership

**Drives initiatives that contribute to societal well-being, positioning the organization as a community leader.**

1. How do you identify and prioritize (social issues/community needs/_____) that align with your organization's mission and values?

2. What strategies do you use to integrate (social impact initiatives/community projects/_____) into your business operations?

3. How do you measure the effectiveness of your organization's (social impact efforts/community contributions/_____) on societal well-being?

4. What role does digital communication play in promoting your organization's (social impact initiatives/community leadership/_____)?

5. How do you engage employees at all levels in (social impact activities/volunteering opportunities/_____) to foster a culture of community involvement?

6. What partnerships do you establish with (local organizations/non-profits/_____) to amplify your social impact efforts?

7. How do you ensure that your (social impact/HR/_____) initiatives are inclusive and benefit?

8. What measures do you take to align your organization's (social impact goals/community leadership objectives/_____) with your long-term business strategy?

9. How do you balance the need for (profitability/business growth/_____) with your commitment to social impact and community leadership?

10. What tools and technologies do you leverage to track and report on your organization's (social impact metrics/community engagement/_____)?

11. How do you communicate the successes and challenges of your social impact initiatives to (stakeholders/employees/_____)?

12. What role does (corporate social responsibility/social impact/_____) programs play in your overall leadership approach?

13. How do you encourage innovation in your organization's approach to (social impact/community involvement/_____)?

14. What success stories can you share where social impact leadership has significantly enhanced your organization's (reputation/employee engagement/_____)?

15. How do you mentor and support other leaders in developing their own (social impact initiatives/community leadership skills/_____)?

16. Looking ahead, what steps will you take to further enhance your organization's (social impact/community leadership/_____) efforts to address emerging societal challenges?

**<u>Dear Valued Reader,</u>**

We kindly ask for your support by leaving a review for our book. Unlike large publishing companies, we rely heavily on the feedback of readers like you.

Your review will not only help us improve and reach more readers, but it will also allow you to share your insights and experiences, contributing to a community of like-minded individuals who are passionate about leadership and personal growth.

To leave your review, please scan the QR code provided.

Your input is invaluable to us, and we thank you in advance for your support!

Warm regards,

Mauricio Vasquez
Be.Bull Publishing

## Unlock Exclusive Resources for Enhanced Leadership (EXCLUSIVE BONUS)

As a special bonus, we are excited to offer you exclusive access to **111 Follow-Up Questions** designed to deepen your conversations, clarify responses, and foster stronger connections with your team and colleagues.

These follow-up questions will help you unlock deeper insights and enhance your leadership effectiveness.

**What You'll Gain:**

- **Enhanced Engagement:** Keep your conversations going and show your genuine interest.
- **Deeper Understanding:** Gain clarity on responses and uncover hidden insights.
- **Stronger Relationships:** Build trust and rapport with your team through thoughtful dialogue.

**Scan the QR Code to Access Your Free Follow-Up Questions:**

# About the Author

Hello, I'm Mauricio Vasquez, and I'm happy to share a bit about myself with you. As a passionate advocate for personal development and professional growth, I strive to make a positive impact on people's lives.

Throughout my career, I have had the privilege of working in diverse fields such as risk management, insurance, e-commerce, and coaching. These experiences have allowed me to create meaningful and lasting change for both individuals and organizations.

I am the proud founder and co-owner of Be.Bull Publishing, a company dedicated to enhancing the lives and careers of professionals. Our mission is to provide high-quality content and resources that inspire growth, learning, and excellence.

In addition to my entrepreneurial endeavors, I specialize in offering risk management and insurance solutions to the mining, power, and renewable energy sectors. My goal is to help these companies safeguard their corporate value, achieve their potential, and positively impact the environment and their communities. As a dedicated professional and life coach, I work closely with fellow professionals to help them achieve better outcomes, lead more fulfilling lives, and become more engaged and effective individuals.

Outside of my professional life, I am passionate about entrepreneurship, marketing, continuous learning, maintaining a healthy lifestyle, mindfulness, and meditation. These interests keep me grounded and motivated in all aspects of my life. I hope this book serves as a source of inspiration and guidance as you embark on your own journey toward personal and professional growth.

Mauricio Vasquez, MBA, B.Eng, M.Mktg, ERM, CRM, CIP, ATC